CLOUDY DAYS

A First Look

PERCY LEED

Lerner Publications ◆ Minneapolis

Educator Toolbox

Reading books is a great way for kids to express what they're interested in. Before reading this title, ask the reader these questions:

What do you think this book is about? Look at the cover for clues.

What do you already know about cloudy days?

What do you want to learn about cloudy days?

Let's Read Together

Encourage the reader to use the pictures to understand the text.

Point out when the reader successfully sounds out a word.

Praise the reader for recognizing sight words such as *are* and *the*.

TABLE OF CONTENTS

Cloudy Days 4

Cloudy Days

It is a cloudy day!
Clouds fill the sky.

Some clouds are
thin and high.

Some clouds are
flat and low.

Some clouds are puffy.

Have you ever seen fog?

Some clouds touch
the ground.
This is called fog.

Clouds can be white.
Clouds can be gray.

Clouds are made up of tiny bits of water. When it is warm, rain falls from clouds.

When it is cold, snow falls from clouds.

Do you like snow?

When it is cloudy,
mountains hide.

Planes fly over the clouds.

When it is cloudy,
we look for pictures
in the sky.

What pictures
have you seen in
the clouds?

19

A cloudy day is fun!

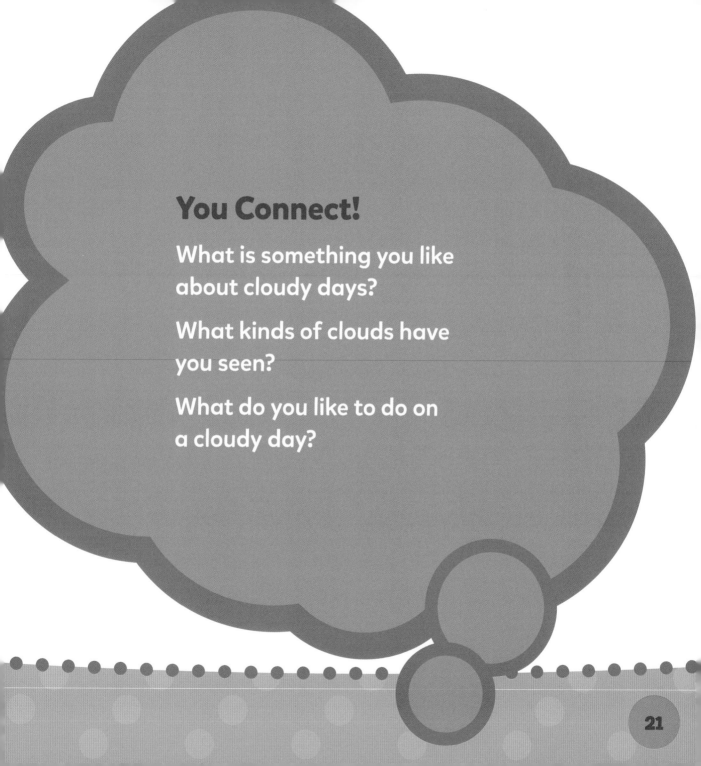

You Connect!

What is something you like about cloudy days?

What kinds of clouds have you seen?

What do you like to do on a cloudy day?

STEM Snapshot

Encourage students to think and ask questions like a scientist! Ask the reader:

What is something you learned about cloudy days?

What is something you noticed about cloudy days in the pictures in this book?

What is something you still don't know about cloudy days?

Photo Glossary

fog

mountains

rain

snow

Learn More

Hodgson, Rob. *When Cloud Became a Cloud*. New York: Rise x Penguin Workshop, 2021.

Peppas, Lynn. *How Do Clouds Form?* New York: Lightbox, 2020.

Peters, Katie. *So Many Clouds*. Minneapolis: Lerner Publications, 2020.

Index

Photo Acknowledgments

The images in this book are used with the permission of: © Erik Gonzalez Garcia/iStockphoto, pp. 4–5; © skhoward/iStockphoto, p. 6; © WLDavies/iStockphoto, p. 7; © SerrNovik/iStockphoto, p. 8; © FatCamera/iStockphoto, pp. 9, 23; © baona/iStockphoto, pp. 10–11; © Mordolff/iStockphoto, p. 11; © nellas/Adobe Stock, pp. 12–13, 23; © kool99/iStockphoto, pp. 14–15, 23; © Jasonfang/iStockphoto, pp. 16, 23; © aapsky/iStockphoto, p. 17; © MediaProduction/iStockphoto, pp. 18–19; © pixdeluxe/iStockphoto, p. 20.

Cover Photograph: © hanapon1002/iStockphoto

Design Elements: © Mighty Media, Inc.

Lerner Publications Company
An imprint of Lerner Publishing Group, Inc.
241 First Avenue North
Minneapolis, MN 55401 USA

For reading levels and more information, look up this title at www.lernerbooks.com.

Main body text set in Mikado a Medium.
Typeface provided by Hannes von Doehren.

Library of Congress Cataloging-in-Publication Data

Names: Leed, Percy, 1968–author.
Title: Cloudy days : a first look / Percy Leed.
Description: Minneapolis, MN, USA : Lerner Publications Company, an imprint of Lerner Publishing Group, Inc., [2024] | Series: Read about weather. Read for a better world | Includes bibliographical references and index. | Audience: Ages 5–8 | Audience: Grades K–1 | Summary: "Some clouds are puffy, some clouds are thin, some carry rain, and some carry snow. With leveled text and engaging photographs, young readers are sure to love learning more about cloudy days"—Provided by publisher.
Identifiers: LCCN 2023002316 (print) | LCCN 2023002317 (ebook) | ISBN 9798765608777 (lib. bdg.) | ISBN 9798765616703 (epub)
Subjects: LCSH: Clouds–Juvenile literature. | Cloudiness–Juvenile literature.
Classification: LCC QC921.35 .L44 2024 (print) | LCC QC921.35 (ebook) | DDC 551.57/6–dc23/eng20230712

LC record available at https://lccn.loc.gov/2023002316
LC ebook record available at https://lccn.loc.gov/2023002317

Manufactured in the United States of America
1 – CG – 12/15/23